A Brief History of the Dissenters

"By whom alone, the precious spark of liberty was kindled and preserved, and to whom the English owe the whole freedom of their constitution."
David Hume

JOSEPH IVIMEY

A BRIEF HISTORY OF THE DISSENTERS

Edited by
Chance Faulkner &
Christopher Ellis Osterbrock

IN PARTNERSHIP WITH

CENTER for BAPTIST STUDIES

A Brief History of the Dissenters
Copyright © 2021 H&E Publishing

Published by: H&E Publishing, Peterborough, Ontario
www.hesedandemet.com

The Andrew Fuller Center for Baptist Studies is under the auspices of
The Southern Baptist Theological Seminary, Louisville, Kentucky

All rights reserved. This book or any portion thereof may not be reproduced
or used in any manner whatsoever without the express written permission
of the publisher except for the use of brief quotations in a book review.

Source in public domain: Joseph Ivimey, *A Brief History of the Dissenters: containing some instances of the advantages they have derived from the government of the present royal family.* London: Wightman and Cramp, 1827.

Cover design by Corey M.K. Hughes
Edited by Chance Faulkner and Christopher Osterbrock

Paperback ISBN: 978-1-77484-028-3
Ebook ISBN: 978-1-77484-029-0

Contents

Who was Joseph Ivimey? ix
   Chance Faulkner & Christopher Ellis Osterbrock

Advertisement xxi

Introduction.. 1
1. Origin and increase 5
2. Sufferings...13
3. Enjoyment of religious liberty..................................... 21
4. Advantages 43

Appendix 67
Timeline 83
Subject Index 89

Who was Joseph Ivimey?

Early Life and Conversion

Joseph Ivimey was born on May 22, 1773, in Ringwood, Hampshire, to Charles and Sarah Ivimey. He was the oldest of eight children, and because his father had "expensive habits" he was not able to secure an education for them. Therefore, in order to support his family, Joseph was compelled into an early apprenticeship in his father's profession as a tailor.

As a young man, Ivimey was well-built and muscular and he was known for his energy, vigour, and for flourishing in athletics.[1] His parents had little interest in spiritual things, so he did not receive a religious upbringing. His first religious impressions came from his aunt while he was apprenticing with his uncle to become a tailor. Shortly afterward, when Ivimey was eighteen, he became distraught over his sins when a

---

[1] George Pritchard, *Memoir of the Life and Writings of the Rev. Joseph Ivimey: Late Pastor of the Church in Eagle Street, London; and Twenty Years Gratuitous Secretary to the Baptist Irish Society* (London: George Wightman, 1835), 6.

A BRIEF HISTORY OF THE DISSENTERS

Welsh Independent minister, Thomas Williams (1761–1844), shared the gospel with him. This conversation with Williams became instrumental in his conversion, for it caused much distress on his conscience and severe lamenting over his struggle with sins. In the winter of 1789/1790, Ivimey was reading the hymns of Isaac Watts and found relief from the lyrics of "Salvation in the cross."[2] After reading stanza three and four, Ivimey saw the glories of the cross for the first time and the clouds of terror were lifted.[3]

> Should worlds conspire to drive me thence,
> Moveless and firm this heart should lie;
> Resolved, (for that's my last defence,)
> If I must perish, there to die.
>
> But speak, my Lord, and calm my fear;
> Am I not safe beneath thy shade?
> Thy vengeance will not strike me here,
> Nor Satan dares my soul invade.

Shortly after his conversion, Ivimey began a friendship with two young men who were members of the

---

[2] Also called "Here at thy cross, my dying God."
[3] Pritchard, *Memoir*, 12.

Who was Joseph Ivimey?

Baptist church in Wimborn, Dorseshire (Dorset)—eight miles from Ringwood. Ivimey attended this church regularly, walking close to six hours each Lord's day. After a short time, Ivimey became convicted of the necessity of believer's baptism—through a sermon by Samuel Stennett (1727–1795)—and was baptized on September 16, 1790, by John Saffery (1763–1825).

In 1794 Ivimey moved to Portsea, where he continued his trade as a tailor. He quickly became known for his integrity and uprightness in his business, maintaining an "unblemished reputation."[4] He married Sarah Bramble on July 7, 1795 and together they had four daughters and two sons. Sadly, only a son and daughter outlived him.

Call to the Ministry

The Senior pastor of Portsea, seeing Ivimey's teaching ability along with his personal piety, first suggested that Ivimey consider the work of ministry and encouraged him to do village preaching. So, in 1803, after

---

[4] Pritchard, *Memoir*, 39.

proving much usefulness, the church at Portsea publicly recognized Ivimey for a Christian minister's work. Shortly after, in September 1803, Ivimey was called to be co-pastor with Robert Lovegrove (c. 1760–1813) at the Baptist church of Wallingford, Berkshire, which Lovegrove built himself in 1794. Ivimey sold his business and devoted himself to full-time work. Shortly after, the church in Eagle Street in London approached him to consider the minister's position there. On May 22, 1804, a call was given and in July 1804, Ivimey and his family moved to London.

As typical of calling a minister at the time, Ivimey went through a probationary period from July to October 1804. On October 21, 1804, he was officially called by the church to be the pastor and ordained on January 16, 1805. His first year proved unusually fruitful, for fifty members were added to the church, and thirty-seven were baptized. Ivimey notes in his diary, "I feel increasing love to the work of ministry and for the people of my charge. I hope nothing will ever render me incapable of preaching the gospel, and if it be the will of God, I hope till my last breath to preach it at Eagle Street."

Who was Joseph Ivimey?

Though it was not long before he would have to taste the bitter cup of trial, when his wife, Sarah, died on January 11, 1807. Providentially, the Lord provided another companion—widow Anne Spence of Eagle Street—and they were married a year later on January 7, 1808.[5] Anne's daughter, whom Ivimey saw as his own child, became the subject of a memoir written for the young women and Sunday school teachers of Eagle Street to exemplify the short but zealous life of Miss Ann Price who died in 1812, at the age of twenty-one.[6]

"To spend and be spent in my master's service"

Following the marriage to his second wife, Ivimey entered a season of much labour. For the next two decades he lived out his prayer, "Gladly will I spend and be spent, in attempting to promote thy honour, and however thou art pleased to appoint."[7] Though unflinching in professional ministry, God used Ivimey to give spiritual vigour to the Eagle Street congregation.

---

[5] Pritchard, *Memoir*, 67.

[6] This memoir is introduced and edited by Ivimey but comprised of the letters and personal writings of the young vibrant woman. Joseph Ivimey, *A Brief Memoir of Miss Ann Price, who died in London, June 16, 1812 in the twenty-first year of her age* (London: the Author, 1812).

[7] Pritchard, *Memoir*, 63.

A BRIEF HISTORY OF THE DISSENTERS

By God's grace, Ivimey saw eight hundred persons added during his pastorate, twenty men ordained to ministry, and four sent to missionary work,[8] along with the establishment of a thriving Sunday school ministry for adults and children,[9] Ivimey was also appointed in 1812 to the Baptist Missionary Society (finding a short but abiding bond with Andrew Fuller), where he helped establish the Baptist Irish Society (as secretary 1814–1833), and became editor of the *Baptist Magazine*.

During his time in fellowship with the elders of the Baptist Missionary Society, Ivimey tasted the richness of both researching and recording history. Herein his usefulness found focused purpose. Through the flourishing relationships within the Particular Baptist community of London, he grew more eager to join this fellowship's gospel impact. His prayers held fast, "It is my ardent desire to spend and be spent in my masters service."[10] By 1810, Ivimey projected to write an encyclopaedic account of his English Baptist forbears through a four-volume work—a work that would take

---

[8] Pritchard, *Memoir*, 314.
[9] Pritchard, *Memoir*, 68. At one point the "Dorcas Society" hosted upwards of 70 regularly attending children.
[10] Pritchard, *Memoir*, 80.

WHO WAS JOSEPH IVIMEY?

him over twenty years to write, completing the task just prior to his death. Along the way he continued to chronicle the contemporary pursuits of those around him, including collecting and editing the Serampore missionary work,[11] writing articles for the *Baptist Magazine*, reprinting pamphlets and tracts from his companions, and chronicling the Baptist mission to the Irish.[12]

As his historical research continued and his volumes of *A History of the English Baptists* met with success, he endeavoured to write biographies of famous Baptists, Protestant Dissenters, and repeatedly contended for the historical Baptist position of strict communion. His concern for Eagle Street, and the wider

---

[11] Francis Augustus Cox, *History of the Baptist Missionary Society, from 1792 to 1842*, vol. 1 (London: T. Ward & Co. and G & J. Dyer, 1842), 273, 280. Ivimey was an original member of the Serampore sub-committee of BMS during the short controversy surrounding the relationship between the leadership of BMS and the missionaries in India as the sub-committee was forming, but Ivimey is notably absent from the role upon the sub-committee's eventual confirmation, yet privy to all the correspondences (293).

[12] Ivimey published a pamphlet, *Triumph of the Bible in Ireland* (1831), celebrating the flourishing work of the Irish Society's 91 weekday schools (16 of which female) "containing more than ten-thousand poor children," 25 evening schools, and six itinerant ministers. See *The Baptist Magazine for 1832*, vol. 24 (London: George Wightman, 1832), 244.

church, was that "No genuine Protestant [should] allow that anything claims his obedience, which owes its origin to human invention, and which can urge no higher authority than ancient tradition."[13] His pen was almost entirely spent upon the necessity of the dissenting church and God's providence in its continuing labour for New Testament practices. He notes, "the English Baptists were the first persons who understood the important doctrine of Christian liberty, and who zealously opposed all persecution for the sake of conscience."[14] What was not spent in Christian history was surely spent all the more in the gospel faithfully preached to his blessed and dissenting congregation.

"To speak of the mercies of the Lord forever"
As he put to print the last volumes of *A History of the English Baptists*, Ivimey once again became a widower. In Anne Spence he had found one "devoted to promote his comfort and usefulness both in his private and

---

[13] Joseph Ivimey, "Preface," in John Chamberlain, *The Constitution, Order, And Discipline of a New Testament Church* (London: J. Barfield, 1820), xvii.
[14] Joseph Ivimey, *A History of the English Baptists*, vol. 1 (London: 1811), vi.

Who was Joseph Ivimey?

public character."[15] However, such tragedy was again matched by the Lord's sovereign blessing. On September 21, 1830, he was married to Elizabeth Gratwick, who was equally devoted to the work of ministry in Eagle Street and the world.[16]

Entering into 1833, Ivimey was aware of his diminished health—he realized he lacked the stamina to do all he felt necessary for Eagle Street. The church hired an assistant minister, today's equivalent of an associate pastor, and sought for pastoral succession if necessary. Robert W. Overbury (d. 1868) was brought on in May. Ivimey was joyful in Overbury, as well in his own ability to prepare for retirement.[17] Though his pastoral ministry was slowing down, he saw more time to consolidate his writing projects and finish those he once had little time for. Weakened in the temporal world, Ivimey spent his last year writing—compelled to share the values of Protestant Dissenterism. A word from one of Ivimey's sermons bears the hope evidenced in his trials: "Let us rather continue in the wilderness with the presence and company of our God, than go

---

[15] Pritchard, *Memoir*, 227.
[16] Pritchard, *Memoir*, 236.
[17] Pritchard, *Memoir*, 269.

A BRIEF HISTORY OF THE DISSENTERS

into the land of Canaan without it. It is as a God of grace he dwells with and accompanies his people."[18] By October of 1833, Ivimey completely relinquished the pastorate to Overbury, and he resigned from the Baptist Irish Society.[19]

On February 8, 1834, after his prolonged health struggles, Ivimey passed into the arms of his Saviour wherein he may "speak of the mercies of the Lord forever."[20] "As a defender of the truth he was fearless, and won many souls to Christ," Thomas Armitage records, "his name is fragrant in all English churches."[21] Though his writing may not be eloquent and is often muddled, his thoughts, passion, and intention was always meant to "promote the general interests of piety, plainness, seriousness, and fervour" in the unity of the church.[22]

---

[18] Pritchard, *Memoir*, 343.
[19] Pritchard, *Memoir*, 281–284.
[20] Pritchard, *Memoir*, 296.
[21] Thomas Armitage, *A History of the Baptists; Traced by their Vital Principles and Practices, from the Time of Our Lord and Saviour Jesus Christ to the Year 1886* (New York: Bryan Taylor & Co, 1887), 587.
[22] Pritchard, *Memoir*, 315.

Who was Joseph Ivimey?

Note from the editors

On October 25, 1809, Ivimey gave an address at Eagle Street reasoning why the Baptist church should be thankful to King George III on his 50th year of reigning. George III was known "for his hatred of persecution"[23] and was tolerant of Protestant Dissenters. Though much could be said of George III politically, toleration amongst the dissenting churches meant far more to the Particular Baptists than anything regarding social economics. This tolerance meant more religious liberty for Dissenters than they had previously experienced. The address was entitled *Motives to Gratitude: An Address Delivered at the Baptist Meeting-House, Eagle Street*, and at the request of the church, was published as a small pamphlet on November 5, 1809. It is this treatise you now hold in your hands.

Ivimey desired for this publication to assist dissenting parents the opportunity to remind and provide their children with the story of the tradition in which they found themselves. The story of holding fast to one's convictions despite persecution. The story of

---

[23] "Anecdotes of the Late King George III" *The Panoplist, and Missionary Herald (1818-1820)* 16, no. 8 (1820): 349.

fighting to be able to worship freely according to one's conscience. The story of promoting "the cause of truth and righteousness in the earth." The story of a people who sought not to receive the doctrines of man, but of God. And by remembering, they would result in "exciting gratitude to God in the hearts, for the many privileges" that the Protestant Dissenters enjoy.

We have sought to provide light edits in a way that keeps the text remaining true to the original publication while making it readable for the twenty-first-century reader. Capitalization and punctuation have been modernized. Archaic spelling has been altered where its meaning is unclear. Scripture references have been provided in footnotes. We have offered citations from other works where they have not been identified. We have also identified persons mentioned in the text in the footnotes.

We pray this publication will be a means in promoting Baptist renewal and an instrument in helping us remember the history of God's work among God's people.

Chance Faulkner
Christopher Ellis Osterbrock
July 2021

Advertisement to the first edition

The discourse from which the following pages are extracted was delivered as an address to the congregation of Protestant Dissenters on the day when His Majesty commenced the 50th year of his reign—a period that will be long remembered as calling forth in a very peculiar manner the nation's gratitude and joy.

The address was published at the request of those who heard it under the title of "Motives to Gratitude." It has certainly been gratifying to the author that it met with so great a share of public approbation. At the request of many judicious persons he has consented to republish it in a cheap edition. The form of it is a little altered, and some additions are made to it; but the substance is the same.

The works from which this little sketch is derived, being large and expensive, the author concluded that many dissenting parents would be pleased with a small compendium which would give their children a general idea of the history of their progenitors. For the use of the young this little work is principally designed; and to them it is respectfully recommended. That it may be honoured as the means of propagating just sentiments on the subject of religious liberty, and of exciting gratitude to God in the hearts of Protestant Dissenters for the many privileges they enjoy, is the sincere wish and ardent prayer of

The Author
London, January, 1810.

Advertisement to the third edition

I had not read over this *Brief Sketch of the History of Protestant Dissenters* for several years. On perusing it again while lately enjoying leisure in the country, I saw no reason for altering it, though at the end of more than seventeen years since it was first written. I was agreeably amused in finding an episcopal prediction of the famous Bill of Lord Sidmouth,[24] which was two years afterwards brought forth, but which was mercifully strangled in its birth. To carry forward the history to the present time, I have written an appendix, in which I have very freely declared my increased conviction of the vast importance of the dissenting principles to promote the cause of truth and righteousness in the earth, and while offering no opposition to the established church, to express my wish most earnestly that my own children may receive and maintain my religious principles as Protestant Dissenters, as the best inheritance they can possibly possess.

---

[24] Lord Sidmouth, or Henry Addington (1757–1844).

Still, however, I hold these principles, only as the best adapted means for promoting the most important end—personal and practical religion. That persons of the most pious and excellent character are to be found in the national church, I have the fullest conviction; but that these valuable Christians must sometimes submit to give up their religious liberty to the will of their ecclesiastical superiors, is necessarily the case; this, however, is a matter for their own consideration. If they admire what I consider to be fetters, they may certainly be indulged in wearing them—I am resolved, divine grace assisting me, still to act strictly upon the divine principle of the Psalmist: "I will walk at liberty, and keep thy statutes;"[25] and never "receive for doctrines, the traditions of men."[26]

Joseph Ivimey
Heathcote Street, Mecklenburgh Square
August 10, 1827.

---

[25] Psalm 119:45.
[26] Matthew 15:9; Mark 7:7.

Introduction

Dissenters are those who separate from the church of England as by law established, and who worship God without those ceremonies enjoined in the ritual, or common prayer.

The grand principles on which they ground their separation are: the right of private judgment and liberty of conscience, in opposition to all human authority in matters of religion; the supremacy of Christ as the only head of the church; and the sufficiency of the holy Scriptures as the rule of faith and practice.

The principal things in the church of England to which they object are: its general frame and constitution as national and established; the character and authority of certain officers appointed in it; the imposition of a stated form of prayer, called the liturgy, and many exceptionable things contained therein; the pretended right of enjoining unscriptural ceremonies; the terms on which ministers are admitted into their office; the want of liberty in the people to choose their own ministers; and the corrupt state of its discipline.[27]

Though these are the principal considerations which justify the Dissenters in maintaining their separation from the national establishment, yet there are now other reasons which induce many to join their communion. These are the corrupt lives of some of the clergy and the erroneous doctrines which are preached in a large proportion of the parish churches. The Dissenters are greatly increased in the present day. It is said, there are some hundred thousand persons of different denominations, probably about two million,[28] and there is abundant evidence of their rapidly increasing.

The exertions which have been lately made in preaching the gospel in the villages and towns where it was not known have contributed to this event. Their

---

[27] See these principles explained and defended in Samuel Palmer, *The Protestant Dissenters' Catechism* (London: J. Buckland, 1772). Samuel Palmer (1741–1813).

[28] This statement includes the Quakers, and the different kinds of Methodists, who, as they separate from the church, are included in the general term Dissenters. The following pages relate only to the three denominations: Presbyterians, Independents, and Baptists.

Introduction

respectability and usefulness as members of the community have fully proved the excellency of their principles, and are a practical confutation of those charges which in fidelity or bigotry may bring against them, either as the heads of families, or as citizens of the state.

1
The Origin of Dissenters
& the causes of their increase

The people whose history we are considering have been known by the names of Puritans, Nonconformists, and Dissenters.

The reformation from popery, which was begun in the reign of Henry VIII,[29] though glorious, was not perfect. Much was accomplished but not all; and even when, in the reign of Edward VI,[30] it was carried much farther, the reformers complain in the preface to one of their service books, "that they had gone as far as they could in reforming the church, considering the times they lived in; and hoped that those that came after them would, as they might, do more."[31] The excellent Edward (the English Josiah) wished to make it

---

[29] Reign 1509–1547.
[30] Reign 1547–1553.
[31] Daniel Neal, *The History of the Puritans, or Protestant Non-Conformists, from the Reformation to the Death of Queen Elizabeth: with an Account of Their Practices; Their Attempts for a Further Reformation in the Church; Their Sufferings; and the Lives and Characters of Their Most Considerable Divines*, 5 vols., 2nd ed. (London, 1732), 1:73.

more perfect but could not accomplish it. In his diary he laments, "that he could not restore the primitive discipline according to his heart's desire, because several of the bishops, some from age, some from ignorance, some out of their ill name, and some out of love to popery were unwilling to it."[32] Yea, even the church herself, in one of her public offices, to this day laments "the want of a godly discipline."

During the bigoted and bloody reign of Mary, many of these godly reformers lost their lives, and many more were obliged to leave the country and settle in foreign parts. Some of these who in the year 1554 resided at Frankfort, differed in their opinion respecting the manner of conducting public worship; those who objected to the introduction of the ceremonies of the church of England, separated from the rest; and laid the foundation for that separation, which continues to the present day.[33] All persons who agreed in sentiment with them were from this period called Puritans.

When Elizabeth came to the throne and avowed herself a Protestant, many of these godly men returned home hoping to obtain such a form of worship as they

---

[32] Neal, *History of the Puritans*, 1:79.
[33] Neal, *History of the Puritans*, 1:108.

Origin and increase

had observed in the best reformed churches abroad.[34] But in this they were disappointed. The queen had modeled the church according to her own fancy, and preferred those only who approved of her establishment. These persons, who were excellent divines and some of the greatest ornaments of the church, desired a further reformation, but not being able to obtain it, petitioned the queen for an indulgence in things indifferent. This being denied, some of the Puritans held a solemn consultation, in which, after prayer and a serious debate about the lawfulness and necessity of separation, they came to the conclusion that,

> Since they could not have the word of God preached, nor the sacraments administered without idolatrous gear, and since there had been a separate congregation in London,[35] and another at Geneva, in Queen Mary's time, which used a book and order of preaching, administration of the sacraments and discipline, which the great Mr. Calvin[36] had approved of, and which was free from the superstitions of the English scr-

---

[34] This was the Presbyterian, of which that at Geneva was the model.
[35] This was held in a warehouse in Bow lane, Cheapside.
[36] John Calvin (1509–1564).

vice; that therefore it was their duty in their present circumstances, to break off from the public churches, and to assemble as they had opportunity, in private houses, or elsewhere, to worship God in a manner that might not offend against the light of their consciences.[37]

This was the era of the separation in 1568, and about four years after a presbyterian synod was founded at Wandsworth.

There was another description of Puritans, who were at first called Brownists, and afterwards Independents. Robert Browne,[38] from whom they descended, resolved to improve upon the principles of the Puritans. Accordingly, about the year 1580, he began to inveigh openly against the discipline and ceremonies of the church of England, which he held up to the people as antichristian. Brown, after enduring great sufferings on account of his sentiments, at last renounced them. But his opinions being founded in

---

[37] Neal, *History of the Puritans*, 1:230, 301, 376.
[38] Robert Browne (c. 1550–1633).

ORIGIN AND INCREASE

truth, obtained very generally so that Sir Walter Raleigh[39] declared in the Parliament house a few years after that the Brownists amounted to 20,000 persons. From the persecutions they had long endured many of them fled to Holland and from thence afterward some went to America.

There was another sect among the Puritans, namely, the Baptists, or as they were generally termed Anabaptists. We find them spoken of under this name as early as 1545,[40] when King Henry VIII, in his speech at the prorogation of his parliament, says, "What love and charity is there among you, when one calls another

---

[39] Sir Walter Raleigh (1552–1618).

[40] This is the first account of the term Anabaptists I have met with. It seems to have been used as a reproachful epithet to distinguish those who wished for a reformation in the church; just as the term Methodist is now applied to all who plead for evangelical truth. It is however probable, that some of the Wickliffites and Lollards were of the same sentiments on the subject of infant baptism as the present English Baptists. A writer in Abraham Rees' edition of *Chambers' Cyclopædia*, and other persons of respectability and eminence, have fully admitted the fact. See Ephraim Chambers, *Cyclopaedia: or an Universal Dictionary of Arts and Sciences*, Supplemented by Abraham Rees, 4 Volumes (London: J.F. and C. Rivington, 1778). Not to be confused with Abraham Rees, *The Cyclopaedia: or Universal Dictionary of Arts, Sciences, and Literature*, 39 Volumes (London: Longman, Hurst, Rees, Orme, & Brown, 1819).

heretic and Anabaptist; and he calls him again Papist, hypocrite, and Pharisee."[41]

From the severities exercised against the Baptists in the reigns of Mary and Elizabeth, their numbers were greatly reduced; many of them also left the kingdom. But an event took place in Holland which tended to revive them, and ultimately to increase them in England. Amongst the banished Puritans, a Mr. John Smyth,[42] who had been a clergyman in the church of England, embraced the sentiments of the Baptists and founded a church at Leyden in Holland. After his death in 1610, many of his people returned home and founded a church in London of the Arminian sentiments;[43] and in a few years after this, about 1633, other churches of the Calvinistic opinion were founded,[44] so that at the beginning of the reign of Charles I. they began to be numerous.

---

[41] John Foxe, *The Acts and Monuments of John Foxe* ed. Stephen Reed Cattley, vol. 5 (London: R.B. Seeley and W. Burnside, 1838), 535.

[42] John Smyth (1554–1612).

[43] Walter Wilson, *The History and Antiquities of Dissenting Churches and Meeting Houses, in London, Westminster, and Southwark; including the Lives of Their Ministers, from the Rise of Nonconformity to the Present Time. With an Appendix on the Origin, Progress, and Present State of Christianity in Britain*, 4 vols. (London, 1808), 1:30.

[44] Thomas Crosby, *History of the English Baptists*, vol. 1–4 (London, 1738), 1:148.

Origin and increase

During the period of the civil wars, in which the Presbyterians gained the ascendency in the state and also in the church; the numbers of the Puritans wonderfully increased, so that they filled the land; and even the Baptists, who were the smallest of the three denominations, about 1646, had forty-seven churches in and about London;[45] and if an adversary, Dr. Featly[46] might be depended on, "they baptized hundreds of men and women in rivulets, about London and in some arms of the Thames." Thus, have we traced the history of the Puritans till they had gained great influence in the country and existed in the three denominations of Presbyterians, Independents, and Baptists, into which they are still divided.

After the restoration of Charles II and the re-establishment of episcopacy, in order to get the Puritans out of the churches, the Act of Uniformity was passed on Bartholomew's day in 1662 which enacted, "that

---

[45] William Wall, *The History of Infant Baptism: in Two Parts. The First, Being an Impartial Collection of All Passages in the Writers of the Four First Centuries, as Make For or Against It; the Second, Containing Several Things to Illustrate the Said History. To which is Added, A Defence of the History of Infant Baptism, Against the Reflections of Mr. Gale and Others*, 4th ed. (London: F.C. and J. Rivington, 1819), 246.

[46] Daniel Featley, also known as Richard Fairclough (1582–1645).

every minister who could not declare his unfeigned assent and consent," to everything contained in the *Book of Common Prayer*, should be turned out of his living. The consequence was, that upwards of two thousand godly men, the lights of the world, left the establishment, and became in different places the founders of churches of each denomination.[47] From this period, all who attended on their ministry were called Nonconformists, which became a general name for all persons separating from the church of England.

In the ever-memorable year 1688, a revolution took place in the kingdom. A few months after, the Act of Toleration was passed, by which all persons separating from the church of England, excepting anti-trinitarians, and Socinians, were relieved from all pains and penalties on that account; and from that period, they have been called Protestant Dissenters.

---

[47] Several of these were Baptists, who had accepted livings under the Committee appointed for the examination of ministers; known by the designation of "Triers."

2
The sufferings of Dissenters

This is an affecting part of English history. It is awful to reflect on the vast quantity of blood that has been spilt, even in England, on account of religion. Happy would it have been if the charge of shedding man's blood, and destroying the followers of Jesus had been confined to Jews and Pagans. But neither these, nor even the Papists, stood alone in this matter. Protestants have shed their brethren's blood and even Puritans have killed each other.

While the bloody Mary and the equally bigoted Elizabeth filled the throne, many of the Puritans were put to cruel deaths. There is one sect amongst them, namely the Baptists, that had the honour of producing martyrs in each of the several reigns of Henry VIII, Edward VI, Mary, Elizabeth, and James I, who were conveyed to heaven in chariots of fire. After the reign of James I, none were burnt at the stake for religion.

A BRIEF HISTORY OF THE DISSENTERS

The hardships which the Puritans endured from the Protestant Star Chamber[48] and the High Commission Court, which have been denominated the English Inquisition, cannot be described. Great numbers of them were confined in loathsome and solitary cells; and in these prisons they died in great numbers, some from want and others of infectious diseases. But the severities did not end here; for in the year 1583, six of the Brownists were proscribed as felons and publicly executed,[49] and others of them were banished their country. Their sufferings arising from imprisonment, confiscation of goods, banishment, and even death, continued to the time of the civil wars when the people, by the arbitrary measures of the king and cruelties of successive prelates, were driven to desperation, so that they subverted eventually the constitution both in church and state.

Impartiality requires that we should not pass over in silence the oppressive measures of the Presbyterians

---

[48] The English Court of Star Chamber (abolished by Parliament in 1641) was a monarch-led council which had gained inquisition-like tactics designed under Anglican authority to discipline and scrutinize dissenting Protestants.

[49] Neal, *History of the Puritans*, 1:389.

Sufferings

when they had succeeded in obtaining the supreme authority. Some of the laws passed at this time, equalled, if they did not exceed, in cruelty, any that had been enacted by Parliaments under the influence of high-church bishops. Happy would it have been if no good man had been entrusted with the magistrate's sword till he had learned that it was only to be used as a "terror to evil doers;" and that, when he attempted to interfere with the sacred rights of conscience, and punished men for their religious sentiments, he invaded the prerogative of God, and exposed himself to the censure implied in our Lord's declaration to his disciples: "The time will come when men shall kill you and think they do God service."[50]

The penal laws passed against the Nonconformists in the reign of Charles II were oppressive to the last degree. The Corporation Act in 1661, incapacitated them from serving their country in the lowest offices of trust. The Conventicle Act, 1663 and 1670, forbad all persons going to any separate meetings for religious worship, when more than five beside the family were present; under very severe fines, to be levied by seizure

---

[50] John 16:2.

of goods, or so many months imprisonment, to be determined, not by a jury, but by the warrant of a justice of peace. The Oxford Act 1665, banished Nonconformist ministers five miles from every corporation that sends members to parliament. And the Test Act passed in that year, made them incapable of all places of profit or trust in the government.[51]

The Oxford Act was passed while the plague was raging in London to such a degree that 10,000 died in a week. The Nonconformist ministers, feeling for the miseries of the sick and dying, entered the pulpits in London which the clergy had deserted. These were the men who must not come (unless upon the road) within five miles of any city or corporation, or any place that sent members to parliament, or any place where they had been ministers, or preached after the act of oblivion. But to all this, these worthy men submitted, rather than violate a good conscience. This was a glorious stand for Christian liberty, which did great honour to

---

[51] Edmund Calamy, *The Nonconformist's Memorial: Being an Account of the Ministers, who were Ejected or Silenced after the Restoration, particularly by the Act of Uniformity, which took Place on Bartholomew-day, Aug. 24, 1662. Containing a concise View of Their Lives and Characters, Their Principles, Sufferings, and Printed Works*, Abridged and Edited by Samuel Palmer (London: W. Harris, 1725), 56.

Sufferings

the Protestant faith, and tended more than a thousand other arguments to convince a licentious and atheistical age of the reality of religion; and entitled them to the high character given them by the immortal Locke,[52] who calls them "worthy, learned, pious, orthodox divines, who did not throw themselves out of the service, but were forcibly ejected."

The sufferings of the Nonconformist ministers were abundant at this time. Those of them who had any maintenance of their own, found out some places of residence in obscure villages, or market towns that were not corporations. Those who had nothing, left their wives and children and hid themselves, sometimes coming privately to them by night. But the majority of them resolved to preach the more freely in cities and corporations till they should be sent to prison. Their difficulties were truly great for the country was so much impoverished that those who were willing to relieve them had generally but little ability. However, it ought to be recorded to the glory of that God whose they were and whom they served, that though they were often in straits, yet they were not forsaken.

---

[52] John Locke (1632–1704).

A BRIEF HISTORY OF THE DISSENTERS

One of them, a noted person among them (says Calamy),[53] said that he never knew or heard of any Nonconformist minister who had been in prison for debt; that though they were brought low, yet they lived comfortably, and maintained their families creditably: many of them bred up their sons to the ministry, in which they were useful; and they at last died in peace, and were laid in their graves with honour.[54]

The Conventicle Act was the cause of great misery to the body of the people. Its penalties were, for every person more than sixteen years of age, above the number specified, for the first offence, to suffer three months imprisonment or pay five pounds; for the second, six months, or ten pounds; for the third, to be banished for seven years, or pay a hundred pounds; and in case of return or escape, to suffer death without benefit of clergy. Their losses in their trades and estates in the space of three years are computed at two million; for so great was the severity of the times, that they were afraid to pray in their families, if above four of their ac-

---

[53] Edmund Calamy (1600–1666).
[54] Calamy, *The Nonconformist's Memorial*, 37.

SUFFERINGS

quaintances, who came only to visit them, were present. Some families scrupled asking a blessing on their food if five strangers were at table.

It was during this period that such men as Baxter, Flavel, Keach, Bunyan, Bampfield, Powell, De Laune, and Gifford, were deprived of liberty, and suffered both in their persons and families.[55] The celebrated Daniel De Foe,[56] speaking of Thomas De Laune, says, "I am sorry to say that he is one of near eight thousand Dissenters who died in prison in the days of that merciful prince, Charles the Second."[57] In the next reign very many suffered both in their persons and property. The policy, however, of James II, who in his zeal to in-

---

[55] Richard Baxter (1615-1691), John Flavel (d. 1691), Benjamin Keach (1640-1704), John Bunyan (1628-1688), Francis Bampfield (1614-1683) Vavasor Powell (1617-1670), Thomas De Laune (d. 1685), George Gifford (1548-1600).

[56] Daniel De Foe (d. 1731).

[57] His crime was preparing a work in answer to a sermon published by a Dr. Calamy entitled, "Ease for Scrupulous Consciences." Mr. De Laune's work was seized at the printer's before it was published. It is well known as "A Plea for Nonconformity." It was condemned by the infamous Jefferies to be burnt with fire. And a fine was imposed on the author, who was sent to Newgate till it should be paid. For want of this sum (66l. 13s.) being raised to pay his fine, this champion of their principles, to the lasting disgrace of the English Dissenters, with his wife and two children, died in prison! "Alas! my brother."

troduce popery published an act of indulgence and universal toleration, put an end to their calamities sooner than their enemies intended, and a subsequent event already mentioned, much sooner than themselves expected.

3
The steps which have led to their enjoyment of religious liberty

The important, and as one would think, the self-evident proposition—that it is the birthright of every man to judge for himself in matters of religion, and be permitted and protected in professing and propagating his sentiments, while they do not interfere with the well-being of society, was at one period considered as the greatest absurdity; and it was many years before it was acted upon in this country. What thousands of lives would have been preserved. How many heart-rending sighs and groans, and how many tears would have been prevented, had this principle been clearly understood. The Papists never dreamed of it, the Reformers would not listen to it, and the Presbyterians were never more shocked than when a toleration of all the sects that differed from them was proposed.[58]

---

[58] Gallio at Corinth and the Town Clerk at Ephesus clearly understood this matter (See Acts 18:12–17; 19:35–41).

A BRIEF HISTORY OF THE DISSENTERS

Of these last it might be said with equal truth as of the Episcopalians, that a rigorous conformity was the idol which they set up; and those that would not worship that idol were deprived of their liberty, and hurried to a jail as wholesome methods to remove their scruples. The very same means were adopted to enforce the use of the directory as had been before of the *Book of Common Prayer*. No person was to use the *Common Prayer* book in any place of worship, or in a private place or family, without incurring a penalty of five pounds for the first offence, ten for the second, and for the third a year's imprisonment.

It is really shocking to observe the spirit these men manifested. When the Presbytery was about to be established, the Independents presented a request to what was called the Committee for Accommodation, December 4, 1645, which was as follows:

> That they may not be forced to communicate as members in those parishes where they dwell; but may have liberty to have congregations of such persons who give good testimonies of their godliness, and yet out of a tenderness of conscience cannot communicate in their parishes, but do

Enjoyment of religious liberty

voluntarily offer themselves to join in such congregations.

To this the Assembly gave a flat denial, December 15, and as signed the reasons why it could not be granted. The Independents, willing to be comprehended in the establishment, went so far as to offer to hold occasional communion with them in their churches, in baptism, the Lord's supper, etc. But all this would not prevail with their brethren to allow them separate congregations. They rather improved this compliance to strengthen their arguments against granting such a liberty.

> If (say they) you can communicate with our church occasionally, once, or a second and third time, without sin, we see no reason why you may not do it constantly; and then separation will be needless. ... As for such a separation as our brethren desire, we apprehend it will open a door to all sects; and though the Independents now plead for it, their brethren in New England do not allow it.[59]

---

[59] Crosby, *History of the Baptists*, 1:185.

A BRIEF HISTORY OF THE DISSENTERS

In order to put an end to all expectation of a toleration, a law was passed on May 2, 1648, called "An ordinance against blasphemy and heresy ... which" says Neal "was one of the most shocking laws I have met with, and shows that the governing Presbyterians of those times would have made a terrible use of their power, had it been supported by the sword."

The Independents of that day, though they pleaded for a toleration, yet appear to have but very imperfectly understood the subject.

> They pleaded for toleration so far (says Neal) as to include themselves and the sober Anabaptists, but they did not put the controversy on a general foot. They were for tolerating all that agreed in the fundamentals of Christianity; but when they came to enumerate fundamentals, they were sadly entangled, as all those must be who do not keep the religious and civil rights of mankind on a separate basis. A man may be an orthodox believer, but deserve death as an enemy to his king and country: and on the other hand, a heretic or Nonconformist to the established religion may

Enjoyment of religious liberty

be a most loyal and dutiful subject, and deserve the highest preferment his prince can bestow.[60]

The Baptists, as far as I have been able to trace their history, appear always to have been enemies to persecution for conscience sake; and never to have aimed as a body to be comprehended in the national establishment.

As early as the year 1589, Dr. Some,[61] a high-church partizan, wrote a treatise against some of the noted Puritans, and took occasion to show their agreement in some things with the Anabaptists. To prove the latter to be heretics, he says, "They say the civil power has no right to make and impose ecclesiastical laws," and "that the high commission court is an antichristian usurpation."[62] By objecting to the magistrate's enacting and imposing laws in the church of Christ, it is evident they understood the principle on which genuine dissent is founded,

---

[60] Neal, *History of the Puritans*, 3:311 312.

[61] Robert Some (1542–1609).

[62] Robert Some, *A Godly Treatise, Wherein are Examined and Confuted many execrable fancies, given out and holden, partly by Henry Barrow and John Greenwood: partly, by the other of the Anabaptistical order* (London: G.B. Deputie to Christopher Barker, 1589). Note the name Robert Soame is also used.

A BRIEF HISTORY OF THE DISSENTERS

which is no imposition. In a work published in 1615, they say, "Every man has a right to judge for himself in matters of religion; and to persecute anyone on that account is illegal and antichristian." And again, in a petition presented to King James I, in 1620, "To persecute men for their conscience sake, is contrary to the law of Christ: these cruel proceedings do no way become the character and goodness of the Christian religion, but are the marks of antichrist, and what they themselves condemn in the Papists."[63]

In an address presented by the Baptists to the king (Charles II), the parliament and people, for toleration, at the time of the Savoy Conference after the restoration in 1660, they say,

> We have written some arguments which we humbly offer to all men, to show how contrary to the gospel of our blessed Jesus, and to good reason it is for any magistrate, by outward force, to impose anything in the worship of God, on the consciences of those whom they govern; but that

---

[63] Crosby, *History of the Baptists*, 1:77, 224. Also, Crosby, *History of the Baptists*, 2:37, 108. This work is entitled, "Persecution judged and condemned."

Enjoyment of religious liberty

liberty ought to be given to all such as disturb not the public peace, though of different persuasions in religious matters. If magistrates (they add), in the days of the gospel, have power, by outward force, to impose anything in the worship of God on the conscience, then all magistrates in all countries, have the same power. Then, if we lived in Turkey, must we receive the alcoran[64]; if in Spain, be Papists; in England, sometimes Papists, as in Henry the Eighth's time, Protestants in Edward the Sixth's, Papists again in Queen Mary's, and Protestants again in Queen Elizabeth's; and so for ever as the authority changes religion, we must do the same: but God forbid! for nothing is more absurd.[65]

Crosby informs us, in reference to this work, that he had been told that while the Presbyterians were pleading hard for such concessions from His Majesty as they thought would bring about an union between them and the Episcopalians, the Lord Chancellor Hyde[66] told them His Majesty had received petitions

---

[64] A reference to the earliest known English translation of the Qur'an, Alexander Ross's *The Alcoran of Mahomet* (London: 1649) from the French *L'Alcoran de Mahomet* (Paris: 1647).

[65] Crosby, *History of the Baptists*, 2:107, 108.

[66] Edward Hyde (1609-1674).

A BRIEF HISTORY OF THE DISSENTERS

from the Anabaptists, who desired nothing more than to worship God according to their consciences. At which they were all struck dumb, and remained a considerable time in silence. "Were Britain, (say some late writers) to erect a statue of gold to the memory of the first patrons of this sentiment, she would but imperfectly discharge the debt she owes to those who have been the source of her wealth, her strength and her glory."[67] The opinion of Bishop Burnet[68] respecting the Baptists in the reign of James II deserves attention:

> The Anabaptists (says he) were generally men of virtue, and of an universal charity: and as they were far from being in any treating terms with the church of England, so nothing but an universal toleration could make them capable of favour or employment.[69]

---

[67] David Bogue and James Bennett, *History of Dissenters, From the Revolution in 1688, to the Year 1808*, vol. 1 (London: William and Smith, 1808), 180.

[68] Gilbert Burnet (1643–1715).

[69] Gilbert Burnet, *Bishop Burnet's History of His Own Time, from the Restoration of King Charles II to the Conclusion of the Treaty of Peace at Utrecht, in the Reign of Queen Anne...*, ed. Thomas Burnet (London: Thomas Ward, 1724), 1:702.

Enjoyment of Religious Liberty

The Presbyterians were on this subject very far behind the Baptists. In 1645, we find the whole body of London ministers, of the Presbyterian denomination, expressing themselves in an address to the Assembly of Divines as follows:

> These are some of the many considerations which make a deep impression on our spirits, against that great Diana of the Independents, and all the sectaries; so much cried up by them in these distracted times, viz. a toleration! a toleration! We cannot dissemble how much, upon the forementioned grounds, we detest and abhor the much endeavoured toleration. Our bowels, our bowels are stirred within us; and we could even drown ourselves in tears, when we call to mind how long and sharp a travail this kingdom hath been in for some years together, to bring forth that blessed fruit of a pure and perfect reformation, and now at last, after all our pangs, and dolours, and expectations, this real and thorough reformation is in danger of being strangled in the birth, by a lawless toleration that strives to be brought forth before it.[70]

---

[70] Crosby, *History of the Baptists*, 1:187.

A BRIEF HISTORY OF THE DISSENTERS

From this we learn, that the Presbyterians never forwarded this great object; and that had not some power superior to theirs prevailed, the blessing was taken up by other hands, and by persons who at that time could demand audience: these were officers of the army. When Oliver Cromwell[71] was embarking for Ireland in 1649, he sent letters to the parliament, recommending the removal of all penal laws relating to religion: and General Fairfax and his council of officers presented a petition for the same purpose: "That all penal statutes formerly made and ordinances lately made, whereby many conscientious people were molested, and the propagation of the gospel hindered, may be removed."[72]

Cromwell has been generally represented as wearing the mask, it seems highly probable that he was sincere in this; for when he possessed the supreme authority, Mr. Baxter says that

> the Protector and his friends gave out that they could not understand what the magistrate had to do in matters of religion; they thought that all

---

[71] Oliver Cromwell (1599–1658).
[72] Neal, *History of the Puritans*, 4:8.

Enjoyment of religious liberty

men ought to be left to their own consciences, and that the magistrate could not interfere without ensnaring himself in the guilt of persecution.

When the Protector found that the parliament would not come into his measures, as to securing to all the liberty of conscience, he thus reproached them at the dissolution in 1654.

> How proper is it to labour for liberty, that men should not be trampled on for their conscience! Have we not lately laboured under the weight of persecution; and is it fit then to make it sit heavy upon others? Is it ingenuous to ask liberty, and not to give it? What greater hypocrisy than for those who were oppressed by the bishops, to become the greatest oppressors themselves as soon as that yoke is removed? I could wish that they who call for liberty now also had not too much of that spirit, if the power were in their hands.[73]

These are noble sentiments! They would have done credit to any head; they are worthy of every

---

[73] Neal, *History of the Puritans*, 4:101.

heart, and raise Cromwell higher as to his views of religious liberty, than any of the ministers who were employed to settle affairs of the church; for, as has been before observed, in the committee appointed to draw up the fundamentals, they differed as to what sentiments should be considered as such. Mr. Richard Baxter,[74] a Presbyterian, proposed, that nothing more should be made necessary than subscription to the apostles' creed? the Lord's prayer, and the ten commandments. But why the apostles' creed? Is it not the composition of men, who were fallible and liable to err? Dr. Owen[75] and the Independents could not go so far; they had so framed their articles as that not only Deists, Socinians and Papists were excluded; but also all Arians, Antinomians and Quakers. Into what difficulties do good men plunge themselves, who usurp the kingly office of Christ, and attempt to restrain that liberty which is the birthright of every rational creature. It is an unwarrantable presumption for any number of men to declare what is fundamental in the Christian religion, any further than the Scriptures have expressly

---

[74] Richard Baxter (1615–1691).
[75] John Owen (1616–1683).

Enjoyment of religious liberty

declared it to be so. It is one thing to maintain a doctrine to be true, and another to declare that without the belief of it none can be saved. None may say this, but God himself. Cromwell, though an usurper, was no persecutor; for in the articles respecting religion, in what was called the Instrument of Government, it was expressly declared, that

> the Christian religion contained in the scriptures be held forth and recommended as the public profession of these kingdoms; and that none be compelled to conform to the public religion, by penalties or otherwise, but that endeavours be used to win them by sound doctrine, and the example of a good conversation.[76]

After the death of Cromwell, and the re-establishment of monarchy and episcopacy, the cause of both civil and religious liberty took a retrograde motion. The sentiments of the sycophants and parasites of Charles II and James II are thus stated by the late Right Hon. Fox:[77]

---

[76] Neal, *History of the Puritans*, 4:100.
[77] Charles James Fox (1749–1806).

A BRIEF HISTORY OF THE DISSENTERS

The character of the party at this time appears to have been a high notion of the king's constitutional power: to which was superadded a kind of religious abhorrence of all resistance to the monarch; not only in cases where such resistance was directed against the lawful prerogative, but even in opposition to encroachments, which the monarch might make beyond the extended limits they had assigned to his prerogative. But these tenets, and still more the principle and conduct naturally resulting from them, were confined to the civil, as contradistinguished from the ecclesiastical polity of the country. In church matters, they neither acknowledged any high authority in the crown, nor were they willing to submit to any royal encroachment on that side; and a steady attachment to the Church of England, with a proportionable aversion to all Dissenters, whether Catholic or Protestant, was almost generally prevalent among them. Thus, as long as James contented himself with absolute power in civil matters, and did not make use of his authority against the church, everything went smooth and easy; nor is it necessary, in order to account for the satisfaction of the parliament and people, to have recourse to any implied compromise, by which the nation was willing to yield its civil liberties, as the price of retaining its religious constitution. The truth seems to be, that the king, in asserting his unlimited power, rather fell in with the humour of the prevailing party, than offered any violence to it. Absolute power in civil matters, under the specious names of monarchy and prerogative, formed a most essential part of the Tory creed; but the order in which Church and king are placed, in the favourite device of the party, is not accidental, and is well calculated to show the genuine principles of such among them as are not corrupted by its influence. Accordingly, as the sequel of the reign of James will abundantly show, when they found themselves compelled to make an option, they preferred without any degree of inconsistency their first idol to the second, and when they could not preserve both Church and king, declared for the former.[78]

The high-church bishops, by preaching the doctrines of non-resistance and passive obedience at last brought themselves into the dreadful dilemma of either resisting the power vested in the chief magistrate

---

[78] Charles James Fox, *A History of the Early Part of the Reign of James the Second; with an Introductory Chapter* (London: William Miller, 1808), 153–156.

and "thus resisting the ordinance of God, and bringing upon themselves damnation," or else submitting implicitly to the dogmas and encroachments of a popish prince. Many of them wished to get rid of such a troublesome head, which caused great pain to the reverend body; they therefore began to alter their tone towards the Nonconformists. When Dr. Lloyd,[79] bishop of St. Asaph, passed through Oswerty, in Shropshire, he sent for Mr. James Owen, the dissenting minister, and ventured to acquaint him with the secret of the Prince of Orange's invitation by some great persons, together with himself; and added, "I hope the Protestant Dissenters will concur in promoting the common interest; for you and we are brethren. We have indeed been angry brethren; but we have seen our folly, and are resolved, if ever we have it in our power, to shew that we will treat you as brethren." Even Archbishop Sancroft,[80] in the circular letter which he sent to the clergy of his province, exhorted them to cultivate a good acquaintance with the Protestant Dissenters:

---

[79] William Lloyd (1627–1717).
[80] William Sancroft (1617–1693).

Enjoyment of religious liberty

That they (the clergy) shall walk in wisdom towards them who are not of our communion; and if there be in the parishes any such, that they neglect not frequently to converse with them in the spirit of meekness; seek by all good ways and means to gain and win them over to our communion; more especially that they have a tender regard to our brethren the Protestant Dissenters; that upon occasion offered, they visit them at their houses, and treat them kindly at their own; and treat them fairly wherever they meet with them; and that they should request them, warmly and affectionately to join us in daily fervent prayer to the God of peace, for an universal blessed union of all reformed church, at home and abroad, against our common enemy.[81]

Such was the language of the church of England when in distress!

This was the state of things when William,[82] the illustrious Prince of Orange, prepared to rescue this unhappy kingdom from the chains of despotism and the horrors of Popery. His first proclamation contained his sentiments respecting religion, dated September 21,

---

[81] Neal, *History of the Puritans*, 4:591.
[82] William Henry III (1650–1702).

1688. It intimates his royal purpose to endeavour a legal establishment of a universal toleration, and inviolably to preserve the church of England in possession of the several Acts of Uniformity, as far as they are consistent with such a toleration.

> Now, the church party (says Bishop Burnet) showed their approbation of the prince's expedition in such terms, that many were surprised at it both then and since that time. They spoke openly in favour of it; they expressed their grief to see the wind so cross; and wished for a Protestant wind that might bring the prince over.[83]

The king, who had relied too much on the clergy's professions of unlimited obedience, was much surprised to find that the prince had been invited over, both by lords spiritual and temporal; and on the landing of the prince at Torbay, November 6, 1588, he soon found that he had lost all his influence, and that he was unable to withstand the excellent William. He, therefore, in a base and cowardly manner left the kingdom, and on the 26th of December the throne was declared to be vacant, and the crown offered to the Prince and

---

[83] Burnet, *Bishop Burnet's History of His Own Time*, 1:784.

Enjoyment of religious liberty

Princess[84] of Orange. They were accordingly crowned king and queen of England at Westminster, the 18th of April, 1689, followed with the joyful acclamations of the whole nation.

Soon after, a bill for the toleration of Protestant Dissenters was brought into the House, entitled, "An Act for exempting their Majesties' dissenting subjects from the Church of England, from the penalties of certain laws." It ought to be recollected, that for the privileges the Dissenters enjoy in consequence of this act, they are not at all indebted to the church of England. Bishop Burnet, who was a low churchman, says that his zeal for this act lost him his credit with the church party; by which it appears they did not like it; and it is very certain that could they have had their will, the Act of Toleration would never have passed.

> Such was the ungrateful return (says Neal) that those angry churchmen made to those who had helped them in distress! For it ought to stand on record, that the Church of England had been twice rescued in 1745 and 1688, from the most

---

[84] Mary Henrietta Stuart (1631–1660).

imminent danger, by men of those very principles for whose satisfaction that would not move a pin, nor abate a ceremony.[85]

It is then to the steady and preserving exertions—the quiet and patient submission—the firm and manly support of constitutional principles, which the Protestant Dissenters have manifested, that we owe the enjoyment of religious liberty; and to this we may add, our civil liberties also. This, the infidel Hume, who hated the religion of the Nonconformists, is compelled to acknowledge: "By the Puritans alone (says he) the precious spark of liberty had been kindled, and was preserved; and to them the English owe the whole freedom of their constitution."[86]

Where then is the propriety of the children of these worthy men being deprived of those privileges which their fathers lost their lives and liberties to procure? Is it just that the Test and Corporation Acts should still remain in force; and thus some of His Majesty's best subjects be prevented from serving him in the lowest

---

[85] Neal, *History of the Puritans*, 4:502.
[86] David Hume, *The History of England from the Invasion of Julius Caesar to the Revolution in 1688*, vol. 5 (London: J.F. Dove, 1822), 120.

Enjoyment of religious liberty

offices of trust, without shamefully prostituting a sacred ordinance, and doing violence to their principles and their consciences. This is a blot in the fairest constitution which the world can boast; and is by all genuine lovers of liberty and of their country, seen and deplored.

4
The advantages Dissenters have derived from the reign of the present royal family

Though the church of England had derived so many favours from the revolution and the accession of William and Mary to the throne of these kingdoms, yet says Neal,

> when the oaths of allegiance and supremacy were tendered, it became visible that many of the clergy took them as oaths of submission to usurpers, during their usurpation, with this reserve, that it was still lawful to assist King James[87] if he should come to recover the crown; and that he was still their king *de jure*, though the Prince of Orange was king *de facto* contrary to the plain meaning of the words.

> But the clergy (says Bishop Burnet), broke through all these fetters to the reproach of their

---

[87] James Charles Stuart, James VI and I (1566–1625).

profession: and the prevarication of so many in so sacred a matter contributed not a little to the atheism of the age, but they had advanced so far in their doctrines of absolute submission, and the Divine right of Monarchy, that they knew not how to disengage themselves with honour and conscience.[88]

The dissenting ministers on the contrary, waited on their majesties with an address of congratulation. This was presented by Dr. Bates,[89] and is expressive of the high sentiments of respect they entertained for their majesties, and the gratitude they felt to God for his distinguishing mercies towards them and the nation. In reply, their majesties assured them of their protection and kindness.

This declaration was inviolably preserved. In a speech made by the king to the House of Peers, March 16, 1689, he intimated his wish that they would leave room for the admission of all Protestants into those places of office and trust that were left vacant by the revolution. By this it was evident that King William was for taking off the test, and abrogating the penal

---

[88] Neal, *History of the Puritans*, 5:75.
[89] William Bates (1625-1699).

Advantages

laws, as far at least as they related to Protestant Dissenters; but this through the influence of the high-church party came to nothing.

The attempts soon afterwards made by bishops Tillotson,[90] Burnet, and others, to obtain a comprehension of the Dissenters in the establishment were also frustrated. The Jacobite party, when this was proposed, said the episcopacy was to be pulled down, and presbytery set up. The universities took fire, and declared against alterations and against all them that promoted them, as men who intended to undermine the church. Severe reflections were cast upon the king himself, as not being in the interest of the church, for the cry of the church being in danger was raised by all the enemies of the government, as that under which they thought they might shelter their evil designs. A convocation was at length called by the request of the clergy, who assured the king that it was intended by them to proceed immediately to the consideration of granting ease to Protestant Dissenters. But the manner in which the debates were conducted proved that they were determined to admit no alterations. King William

---

[90] John Tillotson (1630–1694).

A BRIEF HISTORY OF THE DISSENTERS

being a generous prince, attempted to gain the Jacobite party by heaping favours upon them and therefore submitted to a motley ministry which tormented him during the whole of his reign. Thus, the Tories and the high-church clergy enjoyed the advantages of a glorious revolution, while they acted a most unworthy part towards their great deliverer, and in a most unkind and ungenerous way towards the Dissenters.

These gentlemen never ceased to discover their enmity towards Dissenters when they had power to oppress them. While King William lived, it was impossible to hurt them; but no sooner was Queen Anne[91] upon the throne than they endeavoured to cramp the Toleration by the bill against occasional conformity, which was brought into the house one session after another, till at length it obtained the royal assent in the latter end of the year 1711, under the pretence of preserving the Protestant religion, and of confirming the toleration. The Schism Bill, too, for preventing the Dissenters from educating their children and their ministers, was passed in 1714. Providentially, the very day the act was to take place (August 1) the queen died,

---

[91] Queen Anne (1665–1714). Reigned from 1702–1714.

Advantages

and by this unexpected and happy event all the persecuting designs of their enemies, to their great grief and extreme mortification, were rendered abortive.

It is a very remarkable instance of the care of divine providence over Dissenters, that their great patron and protector King William, and his Parliament, had taken care, in the Act of Settlement, to provide effectually for the Protestant succession, by settling the right to the crown on the line of Brunswick, and in the family of Hanover.[92] To this wise measure the nation is indebted for all that peace and prosperity it has enjoyed since that illustrious family ascended the throne of England, to the exclusion of the Popish branches of the Stuart family.

His Majesty George I landed at Greenwich, September 18, 1714, to the inexpressible joy of every well-wisher to the happiness of his country. The sentiments which animated the Dissenters on this occasion may be gathered from the address presented to His Majesty, by Dr. Williams,[93] in the name of the three denominations. This was published, with His Majesty's

---

[92] This highly important measure, from which such blessings have resulted to the nation, was carried on one division in the House of Commons, by a majority of *one* only.

[93] Daniel Williams (1643–1716), presbyterian theologian.

answer, in the *Gazette* of October 2, 1714, and is as follows:

May it please Your Majesty,

With thankfulness and joy equal to the great occasion, we congratulate Your Majesty's peaceable accession to the throne, and your own, and the prince's safe arrival, the merciful return of many ardent prayers.

When we recollect Your Majesty's descent from the king and queen of Bohemia,[94] those renowned patrons of the Protestant religion, we cannot but adore the divine providence, which has now rewarded their sufferings for that cause, in their royal offspring, with a crown that renders Your Majesty the head of the whole Protestant interest. But Your Majesty's zeal for the same religion, your known affection for the liberties of Europe, and the rights of mankind, with your other celebrated virtues, give us the surest prospect that the blessings of your reign will be as extensive as your power.

---

[94] Elizabeth Stuart (1596–1662) and Frederick V (1596–1632). This marriage coming forth as a means to continue Frederick IV's participation in the Protestant Union, which defended Calvinist and Lutheran states of the Holy Roman Empire against the Catholic League.

Advantages

The parliamentary entail of the crown upon your illustrious house, we have ever esteemed one of the greatest blessings procured for us by our late glorious deliverer King William, of immortal memory. To this happy settlement we have stedfastly adhered against all temptations and dangers. Our zeal herein has been owned to be very conspicuous by those noble patriots who now surround your throne.

We hold no principles, but what do in conscience oblige us to acknowledge Your Majesty for our only rightful and lawful sovereign, and to do everything in our power to support your title and government against all pretenders whatsoever.

Your Majesty's wise and gracious declaration, for which we render our unfeigned thanks, does sensibly relieve us under our present hardships, and gives us ground to hope that as we are inseparably united in interest and safety with all that adhere to the succession and monarchy by law established, so we shall share in that protection and favour which will make us happy with the rest of your subjects.

We shall constantly pray for the long life and prosperity of Your Majesty, for their royal highnesses the Prince and Princess of Wales, and all the branches of your august family. May that

A BRIEF HISTORY OF THE DISSENTERS

God, by whom kings reign, help you so to employ your mighty power and interest, that it may be Your Majesty's glory to protect the Protestant religion, to suppress the profaneness of the age, to heal the divisions of your people, to assert the rights of the injured abroad, and to preserve the balance of Europe.[95]

His Majesty's answer returned to this address was "I am very well pleased with your expressions of duty to me, and you may depend on having my protection."

The royal declaration referred to in the minister's address had been made by His Majesty in council, September 22, 1714, the first time of his sitting in it, in which he said:

I take this occasion also to express to you my firm purpose, to do all that is in my power for supporting and maintaining the churches of England and Scotland, as they are severally by law established, which I am of opinion may be effectually done, without the least impairing the toleration allowed by law to Protestant Dissenters, so

---

[95] Daniel Williams, "The Address of the Three Denominations as Presented to George I by Dr. Williams" in *The Queen's Gazette* (October 2, 1714).

Advantages

agreeable to Christian charity, and so necessary to the trade and riches of this kingdom.

The penal statutes too made against the Dissenters in the reign of Queen Anne were prevented from being carried into effect; and as His Majesty well knew these were occasioned by their steady adherence to the Protestant succession in his illustrious house, against a Tory and Jacobite ministry, procured the repeal of them in the fifth year of his reign, in 1719, till which period they hung over the heads of Dissenters, and some prosecutions had been commenced under them.

His Majesty George II also manifested the same regard to the protection of his dissenting subjects, as the following anecdote from "Orton's life of Dr. Doddridge,"[96] will prove:[97]

No sooner was Dr. D. settled at Northampton, with the pleasing prospect of great usefulness, by his relation to so large a congregation and the increase of his academy than he met with injurious treatment from his neighbours. Not to mention

---

[96] Philip Doddridge (1702-1751).

[97] Job Orton, *Memoirs of the Life, Character and Writings of the late Reverend Philip Doddridge, D.D. of Northampton*, 2 ed. (Salop: J. Eddowes, 1766), 153-154.

some insults which he and his family suffered from the vulgar, through the influence of party spirit, a more formidable attack was made him from another quarter, whence he expected more candour and moderation. A prosecution was commenced against him in the ecclesiastical court by some dignitaries of the Church of England for teaching an academy. Persons of the best sense among the different parties were surprised at the step; and several gentlemen of the established church of considerable rank and public character warmly declared their disapprobation of it. Nay, the very person in whose name the prosecution was carried on, came to the Doctor to assure him of his abhorrence of it; and to know, before it commenced, whether he could with safety to himself, being then churchwarden, refuse to sign the presentment, or in any other way make the matter easy to him. But the clergy seemed determined to carry on the prosecution with vigour; notwithstanding, many acknowledgments which they made of his learning and moderation, and many compliments they personally paid him on that account. This gave him a painful alarm, lest his usefulness as a tutor should have been entirely prevented, or greatly lessened, or he should have been obliged to remove from his congregation to some other part

ADVANTAGES

of the kingdom, where he might have been out of the reach of his persecutors; but his loyal, peaceable, and moderate principles and character, being fairly represented to His Late Majesty by some persons of rank and influence, who had access to him, and were well acquainted with the Doctor; a stop was, by his express order, put to the prosecution; agreeably to the noble and generous maxim he had laid down, that "during his reign, there should be no persecution for conscience sake."[98]

The uniform conduct of this excellent king led Dr. Chandler[99] to compare him to David the king of Israel, in a funeral sermon preached at the meeting in the Old Jewry, November 9, 1760. As the character given by the Doctor of George II is so honourable and so expres-

---

[98] The writer has been lately informed by the Rev. Thomas Taylor, formerly of Carter Lane, Doctor's Commons, who is still living, though upwards of ninety years of age, that he had heard it from the family of Dr. Doddridge, that several prosecutions against that amiable and learned man had been put a stop to by a *noli prosequi* from the king.

It is said that at the period when the celebrated George Whitefield was preaching with such popularity and success in the kingdom, some intolerant persons besought his majesty to interpose his royal authority, and take some means to prevent such crowds from following him; to whom his majesty good-humouredly replied, "I think I must make a Bishop of him."

[99] Samuel Chandler (1693–1766).

A BRIEF HISTORY OF THE DISSENTERS

sive of what were and still are the sentiments of Dissenters towards this illustrious race of monarchs, we transcribe it for the information of our readers.

Speaking of the fears the Dissenters had entertained of losing their liberties at the conclusion of Queen Anne's reign, the Doctor says,

> But our fears were providentially removed by the succession of the present royal family, who, bred up in the principles of protestancy and liberty, and fully convinced of the necessity and utility of mutual forbearance and toleration from the reason of the thing, and the bad consequences that have arisen from the divisions of Protestants in Germany, are so steadily attached to these principles, and have so inviolably adhered to them, as that we have no ground to apprehend the invasion of our rights, or that we shall ever be laid under any farther difficulties for the sake of conscience and religion. His Late Majesty once and again assured us, as Protestant Dissenters, of his favour, inviolably adhered to the assurances he gave us, and told his parliament, June 17, 1715, "I have nothing so much at heart as the preservation of the civil and religious liberties of my people. From these principles I will never deviate,

ADVANTAGES

and in these principles every true Briton will concur."[100]

Without any design to flatter His Present Majesty,[101] it is with the most heart-felt pleasure and gratitude that we record some instances of his royal favour towards his dissenting subjects, and with proud satisfaction say that His Majesty has never violated his declaration at his accession to the throne, "I will preserve the toleration act inviolably."

The first of these relates to an alteration in the laws which has been made in favour of dissenting ministers.

Till the year 1779, the nineteenth of His Majesty's reign, no minister could obtain a certificate, and be entitled to the privileges secured by the Toleration Act, without declaring his approbation of, and subscribing to, the thirty-nine Articles of the Church of England, with the exception of the 34th, 35th, and 36th for the Independents, with part of the 27th for the Baptists, and that part of the 20th which says, "The church hath

---

[100] Samuel Chandler, *The character of a great and good king full of days, riches, and honour. a sermon preached on occasion of the death of His Late Majesty King George II of glorious and blessed memory* (London: 1760).

[101] This referred to His Late Majesty, George III.

power to decree rites or ceremonies, and authority in controversies of faith." But since that period, it is necessary only to make the following declaration:

> A.B. do solemnly declare, in the presence of almighty God, that I am a Christian and a Protestant; and as such, that I believe that the scriptures of the old and new testament, as commonly received among Protestant churches, do contain the revealed will of God, and that I do receive the same as the rule of my doctrine and practice.

The relief which this act provides for those who object to subscribe anything of human composition is very great, as everything human must be necessarily subject to error, and is not likely to be the exact counterpart of any person's sentiments.

Another circumstance of importance related to that useful class of persons, Protestant Dissenting school master, who were not legally authorized till the aforementioned year 1779. There was an act passed in the 13th and 14th of Charles II, which amongst other things enacted,

Advantages

That every schoolmaster, teaching any public or private school, and every person instructing or teaching any youth in any private family, as a tutor or schoolmaster, should subscribe before his or their respective archbishop, bishop or ordinary of the diocese, a declaration to the following effect: "I, A.B. do declare that I will conform to the liturgy of the church of England, as it is now by law established." The penalty for the breach of this law was, for the first offence, three months imprisonment, without bail or mainprize: and for every second and other such offence, in addition to this, to forfeit five pounds to his majesty.

It is rather extraordinary that the Toleration Act made no provision for the repeal of this infamous law; but though it existed, yet during the reign of William and Mary it was not enforced. No sooner, however, was King William departed, but the enemies of the Dissenters were on the alert to manifest their hatred towards them in every possible way. On the news of that afflictive event reaching Newcastle-under-line,[102] the mob assembled and demolished their meeting-house,

---

[102] Bogue and Bennett, *History of Dissenters*, 1:243.

proving, by their excessive joy, that they considered Queen Anne more suitable for their purpose than her illustrious predecessor.

The Schism Bill already mentioned, was framed on the fore-cited bill of Charles II, as its basis; but when that was repealed by George I, no notice was taken of that Act upon which it had been founded; consequently, persons instructing youth were liable to all its penalties, till his present majesty signed the bill, "for giving ease to Protestant Dissenting ministers and schoolmasters."

It would certainly be a great evil were we not at liberty to have our children educated by persons of the same religious sentiments as ourselves. Would it not be very distressing if the poor aged woman who undertakes to teach them the alphabet were to be sent three months to prison and fined five pounds! The idea would be shocking that such a person as Lancaster, who has brought the system of education to such perfection, should be sent to prison for his pains. That the excellent persons who assist in dissenting Sunday schools should be forced either to relinquish this delightful task, or to be deprived of liberty, except they

ADVANTAGES

would sacrifice their principles and declare their unfeigned assent and consent to everything contained in the *Book of Common Prayer*. But that infamous law, by the favour of his present majesty, was repealed, and those dangers are removed; and there is no doubt but the beneficial effects have been and will still be very extensively felt, in the prosperity and happiness of the kingdom.

A still more recent but not less important act relates to the anxiety expressed by his majesty to relieve his Protestant dissenting subjects in Jamaica, from the influence of that intolerant spirit which has for several years prevailed. The history of this affair is as follows:

> The legislature of Jamaica had a second time silenced the missionaries of different religious societies, who had been labouring with the happiest success among the negroes and others in that island. In contempt of the express disallowance of his majesty of their first persecuting act, they had passed another of the same principle, but with restrictions still more comprehensive, and which in effect precluded all teachers, except the clergy of the established church, from attempting to instruct the negroes, etc. The consequence was, that these our oppressed fellow-creatures, and

fellow-subjects composing nine-tenths of the community, were left destitute of all instruction and religious worship, because the few resident clergy of the established church neither do, nor can, extend their pastoral labours beyond the white inhabitants.

The insular legislature knowing that this measure would be disapproved by his majesty, resorted to the trick of engrafting it upon an act to continue the general system of the slave laws, which had been consolidated into a temporary act then just expiring. With a view, perhaps, to some such expedient, they had before substituted this temporary act for a permanent one, which it had repealed. Their agent was consequently led to represent, that if the act of continuation was disallowed, the island would be destitute of all slave law, and that dreadful confusion would ensue. But the committee of Privy Council for matters of trade and plantations, after full discussion, found a way to frustrate this shameful artifice, by disallowing, as they have lately advised his majesty to do, both the act in question and the act of repeal; which had never expressly received his majesty's approbation, though several years in force. The general slave laws

ADVANTAGES

thereby became re-established, and the persecuting clauses only of the act objected to, are in effect annulled.

But the Jamaica legislature, pending this discussion, and by the previous stratagem of delaying to transmit the act for the royal assent, while it had its operation in the island under that of the governor, had, during more than a year, suspended the progress of missions and all religious worship and teaching, by means of them, to the obvious, and perhaps fatal discouragement of those pious undertakings, as well as to the great prejudice of numerous converts recently made, and who were in danger of relapsing again into Pagan darkness and vice.

To prevent, therefore, a repetition of such shameful proceedings in that or other islands, his majesty has graciously issued a general order to the West Indian governors, requiring and commanding that they should not, on any pretence whatever, give their sanction to any law passed concerning religion, until they shall first have transmitted the draught of the bill to his majesty, and shall have received his pleasure respecting it; unless they take care, in the passing such a law, that a clause be inserted, suspending its execution till the pleasure of his majesty shall have been signified upon it.[103]

This circumstance is the more gratifying, as it gives the Dissenters a pledge of the favourable disposition of his majesty towards them at a period when from some events that have transpired, there is cause to apprehend some attempts will be made to abridge their privileges. The old and stale cry, "The Church is in danger," has been repeatedly sounded, and very clamorous addresses to the public and the legislature on the alarming increase of Methodism, have been made, with the hope that government will interfere and prevent the sacred fabric, the work of the wisdom of ages, from falling into ruins. The cause of this alarm is the itinerating labours of the Dissenters in evangelizing those who are absenters from the worship of God in different parts of the country. So determined are some of their enemies to oppose them in this plan, that it is

---

[103] "Extract of a letter from Mr. Spittler, Secretary to the Religious Society at Basle, Switzerland, dated October 18, 1808, addressed to the Rev. C.F.A. Steinkopff, Great Britain," in *The Adviser; or Vermont Evangelical Magazine*, vol. 2 (Middlebury: William G. Hooker, 1810): 156–157.

ADVANTAGES

said a right reverend Gentleman, on a late public occasion, in the West of England, informed his brethren from the altar,

> That as the best way to prevent dissention from the church of England, is to render the Methodist preachers stationary, that method would soon be adopted, and such preachers would be confined to two or three places.[104]

Whatever be the wishes of some gentlemen, we have too high an opinion of the public liberality in general, and of that regard to the free constitution of this country, of which the toleration act is an essential part, which pervades both houses of an enlightened parliament, and especially of that sacred regard to the rights of conscience, which is entertained by our beloved sovereign, to believe that such a subversion of the toleration act will ever be permitted; and could we for a moment suppose it possible, we foresee what would be the inevitable consequences. The ministers of the Gospel who, in compassion to the souls of men, think it their duty to preach in the villages, will not be silenced by

---

[104] "Toleration Act" in *The Evangelical Magazine* 17 (1809): 436–437.

unjust and persecuting restrictions. They will unquestionably persist in preaching whenever they think themselves called to do it; and should severe punishment be enacted, the prisons will be crowded with persecuted Methodists and Dissenters as, in the days of the Stuarts, they were filled with persecuted Puritans and Quakers.

We most sincerely hope that the Magistrates, whose business it is to be a terror to evil doers and a praise to them that do well, will take the advice of Gamaliel, a doctor of the law, and in reference to Dissenters will refrain from these men and let them alone. But while the Dissenters are convinced of the excellency of their principles, we are persuaded they will be determined to preserve and propagate them, as tending to promote the best interests of the nation and the glory of God.

This brief narrative will give a tolerably correct idea of the character of the persons to whose history it refers. It may perhaps awaken curiosity in the young to read the works to which repeated references are made. Should this be the case, there is no doubt but they will receive much gratification and obtain useful infor-

Advantages

mation respecting the principles both of civil and religious liberty. They will discover in the conduct of their forefathers an example worthy of imitation; and by treading in their steps, be an honour to the church and to the world.

Appendix

The quotation made from a charge delivered to the clergy of a western diocese in 1809 by its bishop, proved that his Grace was well acquainted with the project of Lord Sidmouth then in embryo, for rendering the dissenting ministers respectable and orderly. This measure was in the year 1811 brought into the House of Lords, in his lordship's ever-memorable bill, memorable both for its persecuting enactments and for its shameful defeat.

This hateful measure was designed to alter the provisions of the Toleration Act, and to abridge the liberties of Protestant Dissenters. It proposed that no persons should be capable of exercising the office of a minister, who did not first obtain a certificate of recommendation from six respectable dissenting housekeepers, and then a license from some county magistrate—that all settled ministers and pastors of churches should confine their labours to their own respective congregations. It also enacted fines and imprisonments as the penalties for disobedience, etc.

A BRIEF HISTORY OF THE DISSENTERS

It was read the first time on the 9th of May, 1811. The alarm it spread among all classes of Dissenters, especially the Wesleyan Methodists, was very great. Petitions to the amount of several thousands, before the second reading, were poured into the house, and these, brought by loads in their arms, were presented by the opposition Lords, Erskine, Grey, Lansdowne, Stanhope, Howard and others.[105]

I was in the house on that occasion, and had the happiness of witnessing the defeat of this hostile measure to our rights and liberties, Thursday, May 23.

It was not known at the beginning of the evening how it would terminate, as the government had not avowed its sentiments on the measure. After the presentation of the petitions, Lord Sidmouth proposed the second reading of the bill, disavowing most positively any design to injure the Protestant Dissenters. This was the more inexcusable because his Lordship had been made fully acquainted by a deputation from the dissenting deputies for defending their civil rights with their strong objections to the provisions of his bill,

---

[105] James St. Clair-Erksine (1762–1837), Charles Grey (1764–1845), Henry Petty-Fitzmaurice, Marquis of Lansdowne (1780–1863), Philip Henry Stanhope (1781–1855), Kenneth Howard (1767–1845).

Appendix

and the impossibility, should it pass into law, of their being governed by its enactments. No sooner had his Lordship concluded, than the premier, Lord Liverpool, rose in his seat. His Lordship lamented that the Dissenters should have mistaken the nature of the bill, and of the design of his noble friend, etc., but said "The Toleration laws he was ready to say were matters on which he thought the legislature should not touch, unless it were from matters of great paramount necessity." He concluded by advising his noble friend to withdraw his motion.[106] This advice, however, Lord Sidmouth refused to take. The speeches delivered by the peers, who were entrusted with the Dissenters' petitions, did them very great credit. Nor should the liberal speech of Dr. Sutton,[107] the present Archbishop of Canterbury, be overlooked or forgotten. His Grace declared

---

[106] The following conversation took place between the writer, and as he supposes, a reporter for a newspaper. When Lord Liverpool had sat down, the gentleman said, "There is an end of the bill." I said, "Why do you thus conclude?" He replied, "Did you not hear what Lord Liverpool said?" "And do you not," said I, "see all the bishops on the bench. Will they not, think you, vote all of them for the measure?" He replied archly, Perhaps they might, were there no Archbishopricks."

[107] Charles-Manners Sutton (1755–1828).

A BRIEF HISTORY OF THE DISSENTERS

his abhorrence of every species of persecution, and while he lamented the errors, as he thought them, of the Protestant Dissenters from the church of England, he admitted that they had a full right to the sober and conscientious profession of their own religious opinions. The sacred writings were allowed by all Protestants to be the great standard of religious doctrine, but the interpretation of them was liable to error. Uniformity of religious belief was not to be expected, so variously constituted were the minds of men; and consequently religious coercion was not only absurd and impolitic, but for all good purposes impracticable. He thought it would be both unwise and impolitic to press this bill against the consent of the Dissenters, etc.[108]

The rejection of this bill, and some circumstances connected with it, led the Dissenters, principally the Wesleyans, to follow up the success by requesting his majesty's ministers to improve the Act of Toleration. It is due to Lord Liverpool and his worthy colleagues to say, that they promptly and kindly attended to this application, and what is known as the "New Toleration

---

[108] Samuel Chandler, *The History of Persecution: From the Patriarchal Age to the Reign of George II* (Hull: J. Craggs, 1813), 463.

Appendix

Act," enlarging and confirming the privileges of Protestant Dissenters, was soon after obtained.

Another serious attack was made upon their rights and privileges in the year 1820. This was by the proposed Education Bill of Mr. Henry Brougham, M.P.[109] for Winchelsea. Its original shape indicated that it had been cast in the moulds of the Schism Bill, and of the Test and Corporation Acts, the *Book of Sports*, etc. It provided that all poor children, who would receive a gratuitous education, should attend the established church; having the afternoon of the Lord's day for play and diversion, and that the masters should be parish clerks appointed by the magistrates, the schools to be under the sole management of the residing clergyman, rector, or curate. A most obnoxious measure in violation of all the previous principles of the gentleman who had drawn the sketch of the bill, and of all his professions of respect for the Protestant Dissenters. To one of those who strongly remonstrated with him against the principle of the bill, he replied, "Your poor do not object to receive parish relief, because it comes through the hands of overseers who are churchmen." Mr.

---

[109] Henry Broughman (1778–1868).

A BRIEF HISTORY OF THE DISSENTERS

Brougham appeared to be resolved on attempting to carry his measure; but whether from the powerful opposition made to it by all classes of Dissenters, or from the land holders objecting to an additional burden being laid upon their tenantry for the support of the schools, or whether his majesty's ministers had intimated they would afford the Dissenters their protection, the bill, after all the expense and trouble occasioned to the nation by it, was wisely withdrawn. But for this event, the Dissenters throughout the united empire would have petitioned the Legislature against it as vigorously and as numerously as at the time of Lord Sidmouth's bill.

From that period no hostile measure against us has been attempted by any member of either branch of the legislature. Nor have we any fear for our liberties, while the liberal sentiments of his majesty and of the royal family respecting us are so well known; we feel confident the present monarch will never suffer his coronation oath, nor his declaration to preserve the Toleration Act inviolable, to be broken or impaired. It ought to be recorded to the honour of the Protestant Dissenters, and as affording proof that they have no wish to interrupt or oppose the church of England, that when it was

Appendix

proposed by the Chancellor of the Exchequer[110] to vote on two separate occasions one million and a half of money from the public treasury for building new churches, they did not attempt to offer any opposition to the measure, thus submitting to contribute their proportion towards erecting churches for the established church, and towards the support of an increased number of clergymen, in addition to erecting all their own meeting-houses and chapels, and supporting all their own ministers.

On the occasions referred to, the government seem to have adopted as a maxim (what there is reason to think is the watch-word of the present Bench of Bishops) "As to the Protestant Dissenters, say nothing at all about them!"[111] Well, we must endeavour to submit to this affected ignorance of our existence, and of our prosperity. We will still, however, endeavour to prove ourselves worthy of the protection afforded us by the government, and should our rights as citizens be still unjustly withheld from us, and the Test and Corpora-

---

[110] Nicholas Vansittart (1766–1851), held office May 1812–January 1823.

[111] This the writer has been credibly informed was said by an evangelical bishop not long since.

tion Acts be permitted to exist the disgrace of the statute book for profaneness and oppression, we will quietly submit, rejoicing that, as to the most extensive liberty of conscience, "we sit each man under his vine and fig tree, none making us afraid."[112] I am of opinion that the national church never presented such a powerful rivalry to the Dissenters as at the present time. The large number of evangelical clergy, and many of them of most splendid and popular talents as preachers—the increased respectability even of those who are by themselves called the orthodox, as well as the numerous, handsome and convenient churches which have been lately erected—the regard paid to learning and reputation in filling the vacant sees, etc. all tend to raise the established church to a higher degree of religious elevation than she ever before enjoyed. All these considerations, however, leave the matter as to the grounds of our dissent unchanged, and the importance of our principles as to the spiritual nature of Christ's kingdom untouched. And while we rejoice "if Christ be preached," and especially if it be "from good will,"[113] we shall feel ourselves called upon to redouble our zeal to preach

---

[112] Micah 4:4.
[113] Philippians 1:15.

Appendix

and propagate by every possible way within our power those scriptural sentiments as to the sole headship of Christ in his church; the imprescriptible right of private judgment; the unalienable freedom of conscience, and the entire sufficiency of the Scriptures, which led our forefathers Tyndale[114] and Frith,[115] and their followers to separate themselves from the established popish church of England—which prevented John Fox[116] and others from subscribing its reformed Articles—and Cartwright[117] and the Puritans from approving its Rubric; which influenced the noble army of martyrs, on black Bartholomew day, to refuse conformity to all and everything contained in the *Book of Common Prayer*, and in common with all other Dissenters, to suffer throughout the reigns of the restored Stuart kings every species of persecution. To the rigid and steady avowal of these our principles during more than three centuries, may the nation's political and commercial prosperity be distinctly traced; nor is it at all probable that the national church would ever have attained to its present character as a religious institution, but for the rivalry which

---

[114] William Tyndale (1494–1536).
[115] John Frith (1503–1533).
[116] John Foxe (1516/1517–1587).
[117] Thomas Cartwright (1535–1603).

the Protestant Dissenters have afforded. Most sincerely do I hope that the spirit of laxity called Catholicism, which has of late years been introduced among us by the specious charity of those Dissenters who have taken the lead in Bible Associations and other similar religious institutions, comprehending church men and all sects of Dissenters, may not lead our young people to undervalue. the importance of principles for which our noble progenitors parted cheerfully with their property, their liberties, and their lives. It is one affecting sign of the times, in regard to the spirit and principles of dissent, that even the sons of our ministers and other leading and influential persons should have been induced by any considerations to have conformed to the established church. But if the superior worldly respectability of the establishment lead the fathers to look down with indifference, and to speak with contempt of the dissenting body, it is no great marvel if rich livings and prebendaries stalls should prove too powerful temptations to be resisted by their sons. The principles of dissent are purely scriptural, those of the establishment partly human, because it is avowedly built upon the decrees of the first four general Councils. And let it be recollected, these Acts of Councils and other human

Appendix

appointments are imposed upon the faith of all her members; nor are they left even at liberty to choose their own spiritual instructors. Should we not then ourselves resolve to "Stand fast in the liberty wherewith Christ has made us free,"[118] and to exhort our children, that they may teach it to their children; that whenever they are required to observe anything in matters of religion that claims no higher authority than human tradition, or man's invention, they should boldly and unhesitatingly reply, whatever they may lose by it, or suffer on account of it, "Whether it be right to obey God rather than men, judge ye."[119]

The present condition of the Dissenters as to numbers, and as to respectability in regard to property, may be in some measure judged of from the very large sums of money raised by voluntary contributions (in addition to supporting their ministers)—for promoting education by their numerous Sunday schools and public seminaries and universities; for sending the gospel to the heathen, and in the erection of convenient and some of them very large and even elegant places of worship. A popular writer belonging to the church of England, a

---

[118] Galatians 5:1.
[119] Acts 4:19.

A BRIEF HISTORY OF THE DISSENTERS

few years ago described "Dissenterism as the religion of barns,"[120] and another writer of the same school lately called their meeting-houses "long tiled barn looking places." I consider these expressions in the light of flights of rhetoric, and therefore, as indicating no more than the envious spirit of their respective authors; but if any person has been led away by them to conceive of the meeting-houses (or, as they are now generally called, chapels), as being mean and inconvenient buildings, let him view all, and especially some of the chapels in London, and then visit Bristol, Liverpool, Manchester, Birmingham, Portsea, etc., and he will soon find they lose nothing in respectability of appearance, even in comparison with the churches in general (excepting the cathedrals) of the Established Church. The Dissenters, as a body, have during the present year renewed their exertions to procure the repeal of the Test and Corporation Acts, and a gentleman of noble descent (Lord John Russell)[121] had given notice of his intention to bring the subject before the House of Commons, on a day fixed for that purpose. But in the interim

---

[120] John William Cunningham, *The Velvet Cushion* (London: T. Cadell and W. Davies, 1814), 17.

[121] John Russell (1792–1878).

Appendix

a new administration was formed, and the Premier, the late Mr. Canning,[122] declared his determination to prevent their repeal. It has been said too that a most liberal supporter of all liberal measures told the Dissenters, "that if they persevered in their application to Parliament, he would himself move the previous question and thus prevent the discussion." The consequence was, that the Committee appointed in London requested Lord John Russell to withdraw his motion, which I have been told he most reluctantly complied with.

In conclusion, I would take the liberty to exhort the Dissenters to be more concerned to improve their religious liberty than to be anxious for obtaining civil advantages. If they are contented with protection from the Government they may be happy; if they are restless because they have not honours and immunities from the State they will be miserable. The opinion of the writer has long been, and he sees no reason from any recent changes in the administration to alter it, that while the Government consider it necessary for its own

---

[122] George Canning (1770–1827).

safety to maintain the Church of England as the endowed and established sect, all other sects of Protestants must pay as the price for protection exclusion from all places of power, honour, and emolument in corporations and places under the Crown. Unless, indeed, they choose to run the risk, during the space of a few weeks, of paying £500 for having accepted an office which they are proscribed from filling—or of accepting a pardon for such offence by the Bill of Indemnity, annually passed for the relief of such transgressors.

On the subject of the laws which bear heavy upon all Dissenters from the establishment, I adopt the sentiments of an eminent Nonconformist minister, the Rev. Philip Henry.[123] His biographer, the celebrated Matthew Henry,[124] speaking of his father, in regard to the eventful year 1685, says

> The subject of debate in the nation at this time was concerning the repeal of penal laws and tests. Mr. Henry's thoughts were, as to the penal laws, that if those against the Dissenters were all repealed, he would rejoice in it, and be very

---

[123] Philip Henry (1631–1696).
[124] Matthew Henry (1662–1714).

Appendix

thankful both to God and man; for he would sometimes say, without reflection upon any, that he could not but look upon them as a national sin; and as for those against the Papists "If our lawgivers," said he "cause to repeal them in a regular way, I will endeavor to make the best of it, and say 'The will of the Lord be done.'"

Timeline of the Protestant Dissenters

as outlined in the 300-year span of this *Brief History*

1545	Henry VIII (1491–1547)
	Dissenting sects lumped together as Anabaptists and thereby persecuted by the state church.
1568	Wandsworth first established Presbyterians in England.
1580	Brownists emerge. Hold that baptism alone does not save or bring a person into the church. The body of believers are to elect their own officers. Membership is to be bound by a voluntary covenant not by residence or birth.
	John Smyth founded Baptist church in Leyden, Holland
1610–1633	Emergence of Baptist churches in London. Transplanted from Holland.
1644	First London Baptist Confession of Faith

1642–1651	English Civil War
1653–1660	English Commonwealth under Oliver Cromwell
1660	Dissenting groups thrived. Dissenting Academies begin emerging.
1661	Charles II is invited back as monarch in the English Restoration.
	Savoy Conference organized to limit dissention. Precursor to the Act of Uniformity.
	Corporation Act: Dissenters were to be held in lowest offices of trust.
1662	Act of Uniformity came into effect on the anniversary of the St. Bartholomew's Day Massacre (1572).
1665	Five Mile Act (Oxford Act). Penalized expelled Nonconformist ministers from living or serving within five miles of any place of worship from where they once served. Penalty could be reconsidered by swearing oath to Church of England, State, or *Book of Common Prayer*.

1663 & 1670	Conventicle Act. All worship is restricted to that ordained under the Church of England's leadership.
1673	Test Act. Only those taking communion, as ordained by the Church of England, eligible for public employment; those refusing attendance to be penalized.
1688	Act of Toleration. Granted freedom to Dissenters to worship in their own meetinghouses.
	Second London Baptist Confession of Faith
1689	William, Prince of Orange resolves to encourage the toleration of Dissenters within the House of Commons.
1701	Act of Settlement. Protestants alone to hold royal offices.
1711	Anne becomes queen, and threatens toleration efforts for Dissenters.
1714	Schism Act. Dissenters are forbidden to hold schools or tuition.
	George I takes throne. Dissenters present *Address of the Three Denominations* to George I.

1719	Schism Act repealed
1727	Indemnity Act. Relieves Dissenters from the oaths of the Test and Corporations Acts.
1753	Clandestine Marriages Act. Only those ministers in the Church of England could perform binding marriage ceremony.
1773	Under George III, both Whig (Charles James Fox) and Tory (William Pitt) parties petition for relief and liberty to Dissenters.
1779	Nonconformist Relief Act. Dissenters were permitted to preach and teach, under condition of oath of oaths of allegiance.
1792	Baptist Missionary Society is founded.
1804	Baptist Education Society. Stepney Academy would be established in 1810.
1809	Joseph Ivimey presents *Motives to Gratitude* at Eagle Street Meetinghouse.
1811	Lord Sidmouth's Bill against Dissenting ministers is refused.
1814	Baptist Irish Society established.

1820	George IV takes throne.
	Education Bill (similar to Schism Act) brought before Parliament by Henry Broughman. Withdrawn following immense opposition.
1828	Test and Corporation Acts officially repealed.
1830	Death of George IV

Subject Index

Act of Settlement, 45
Act of Toleration, 12, 39
Act of Uniformity, 11, 37
Addington, Henry. *See*
　Lord Sidmouth
America, 9
Anabaptists, 9, 24, 25, 27
Anne, 44
Antinomianism, 32
Apostles' Creed, 32
Arianism, 32
Arminianism, 10
Bampfield, Francis, 19
Banishment, 10, 14, 16, 18
Baptism, 9, 23
Baptists, 2, 9, 10, 12, 13, 25,
　26, 28, 29, 54
Bartholomew's Day, 11
Bates, William, 42
Baxter, Richard, 19, 30, 32
Bigotry, 3
Bill of Indemnity, 78
Blasphemy, 24
Bloody Mary. *See* Mary I
Book of Common Prayer,
　11, 22, 57
Book of Sports, 69
Brougham, Henry, 69

Browne, Robert, 8
Brownists, 8, 14
Bunyan, John, 19
Burnet, Gilbert, 28, 38, 39,
　41, 43
Burnett, Gilbert, 28
Calamy, Edmund, 16, 18, 19
Calvin, John, 7
Calvinism, 10
Canning, George, 77
Cartwright, Thomas, 73
Catholicism, 34
Chandler, Samuel, 52, 68
Charles I, 10
Charles II, 11, 15, 19, 26, 33,
　55, 56
Church of England, 1, 6, 8,
　10, 12, 28, 34, 37, 39, 41,
　50, 54, 55, 61, 68, 71, 73,
　75, 77
Committee for
　Accommodation, 22
Conscience, 1, 15, 16, 22,
　25, 26, 27, 31, 42, 47, 51,
　53, 62, 72, 73
Controversy, 24
Conventicle Act, 15, 18
Corporation Act, 15

A Brief History of the Dissenters

Court of Star Chamber, 14
Cromwell, Oliver, 30, 31, 32, 33
Crosby, Thomas, 27
De Foe, Daniel, 19
De Laune, Thomas, 19
Debt, 18, 28
Deism, 32
Despotism, 37
Disease, 14
Doddridge, Philip, 49, 51
Education, 44, 55
Education Bill, 69
Edward VI, 5, 13, 27
Elizabeth I, 5, 6, 9, 13, 27
English civil wars, 10, 14
Episcopalians, 22, 27
Established Church, 23, 50, 58, 69, 71, 72, 74
Fairclough, Richard. *See* Featley, Daniel
Featly, Daniel, 11
Flavel, John, 19
Fox, Charles James, 33
Foxe, John, 73
Frederick V, 46
Frith, John, 73
George I, 45, 56
George II, 49, 52, 68
George III, 53
Gifford, George, 19
Grey, Charles, 66
Hanover, 45
Henry VIII, 5, 9, 13, 27

Henry, Matthew, 78
Henry, Philip, 66, 78
Heresy, 24
High Commission Court, 14
Holland, 9, 10
Howard, Kenneth, 66
Hume, David, 3, 40
Hyde, Edward, 27
Imprisonment, 14, 16, 17, 18, 19, 22, 55, 57
Independents, 2, 8, 11, 22, 23, 24, 29, 32, 54
Ivimey, Joseph, 6, ix, 24
Jacobite, 43, 44, 49
James I, 13, 26
James II, 20, 28, 33
James VI, 41
Jews, 13
Keach, Benjamin, 19
Liturgy, 1
Lloyd, William, 36
Locke, John, 17
Lollards, 9
Lord Sidmouth, 23, 65, 66, 67, 70
Lord's Supper, 23
Martyrdom, 13, 73
Mary I, 6, 7, 9, 13, 27
Methodism, 2, 9, 61, 62, 66
Nonconformists, 5, 12, 15, 36, 40
Owen, James, 36
Owen, John, 32

Subject Index

Oxford Act, 16
Palmer, Samuel, 2
Persecution, 13, 25, 30, 31, 51, 68, 73
Petty-Fitzmaurice, Henry, 66
Plague, 16
Popery, 5, 6, 20
Powell, Vavasor, 19
Prayer, xxii, 1, 7, 19, 32, 37, 48
Presbyterianism, 2, 7, 10, 11, 15, 21, 24, 27, 28, 29, 32
Prince of Orange. *See* William III
Protestant Star Chamber, 14
Protestantism, xxi, xxii, 23, 2, 5, 12, 14, 34, 36, 38, 39, 40, 43, 48, 49, 54, 55, 56, 65, 69, 70, 71
Puritans, 5, 6, 7, 8, 9, 10, 11, 13, 14, 25, 30, 40, 42, 62, 73
Quakers, 2, 32, 62
Queen Anne, 28, 49, 52, 56
Raleigh, Walter, 9
Reformers, 5, 6, 21
Religious liberty, xxii, 24, 2, 21, 31, 33, 40, 63, 77
Russell, John, 76, 77
Sancroft, William, 36

Savoy Conference, 26
Schism Bill, 46, 58, 71
Smyth, John, 10
Socinians, 12, 32
Some, Robert, 25
St. Clair-Erksine, James, 66
Stanhope, Philip Henry, 66
Stuart, Elizabeth, 46
Stuart, Mary Henrietta, 38
Stuarts, 41, 45, 62, 73
Sunday schools, 57, 75
Sutton, Charles-Manners, 67
Test Act, 16
Test and Corporation Acts, 40, 71, 74, 78
Tillotson, John, 43
Toleration, 20, 21, 24, 26, 28, 29, 37, 39, 44, 49, 52, 61, 62
Toleration Act, 53, 54, 55, 61, 62, 65, 69, 70
Tory, 35, 49
Tyndale, William, 73
Vansittart, Nicholas, 71
Village preaching, 2
Wandsowrth Presbytery of 1572, 8
Wickliffites, 9
William III, 37, 41
William IV, 43, 44, 45, 47
Williams, Daniel, 46
Women, 11

Editors

CHANCE FAULKNER is the co-founder and Editorial Director of H&E Publishing. He serves as a Junior Fellow of the Andrew Fuller Center for Baptist Studies, and as Managing Editor for Union Publishing. He is married to Mary Austin, and together they have five children (Titus, Ezra, Frances, Glory, Lucy). He worships at Braidwood Bible Chapel in Peterborough, Ontario.

CHRISTOPHER ELLIS OSTERBROCK is pastor of First Baptist Church of Hamilton, Ohio. He is married to Emily, a devoted mother to their three daughters (Ruth Aurelia, Edra Althea, and Hadassah Augusta). Alongside service to his local church, much of his time is spent toward Baptist church history, spirituality, and Christian education. He also serves H&E as Project Manager of reprints.

www.ingramcontent.com/pod-product-compliance
Lightning Source LLC
Chambersburg PA
CBHW070923080526
44589CB00013B/1412